Years 1-2

Badger

Sentence Writers

TEACHER BOOK WITH COPYMASTERS & CD

Activities and games to help children write better sentences

Pie Corbett and Ann Webley

You may copy this book freely for use in your school.
The pages in this book are copyright, but copies may be made without fees or prior permission provided that these copies are used only by the institution which purchased the book. For copying in any other circumstances, prior written consent must be obtained from the publisher.

Badger
LEARNING

INTRODUCTION

Badger Sentence Writers for Years 1-2 has been produced to help you teach children in KS1 about the nature of sentences and the words used within them. (Some of the early activities will also be useful in Foundation Stage.) It will help children to say and write sentences more clearly and with greater independence. Each activity is intended as a quick starter rather than a whole lesson.

THE CONTEXT

It is important that children are familiar with the content of a sentence if they are going to investigate it or to put different parts together to create a new construction. As a result, we have used well known traditional tales and nursery rhymes as the context. You will know whether your own class is familiar with a story so you will be able to adapt the resources as appropriate – or, indeed, read a story or rhyme to the children prior to the activities in this book.

You will also be able to adapt and extend all the activities by altering and adding to the Word files on the CD. This means that you can create fiction and non-fiction sentences, based on the same learning objectives, but related to stories you are reading or topics you are covering in other areas of the curriculum.

THE APPROACH TO LEARNING

We intend this to be a multi-sensory approach.

Kinaesthetic

Small children learn best by actively taking part in the learning. Therefore, we have designed a number of Copymasters to be made into games. Some become small cards, but others might work best on larger strips of card after the Copymasters have been enlarged. You will be able to play the games as a class, with children sometimes moving around the room to join parts of a sentence together. You will also be able to repeat the games as often as needed with small groups in order to revise or reinforce.

Visual

Children are helped by the use of colour. This book is printed in black and white but the teacher's notes suggest opportunities to use highlighting in colour to draw attention to the learning objective. The CD is already in colour where appropriate and you will be able to replicate this with your own sentences and passages of text.

Auditory

We have found that using actions and noises for punctuation helps children to internalise the concept of a sentence and the different kinds of sentences that they meet. Copymasters 47-48 show the actions and noises used in this book. You might like to create a chart of your own, adding punctuation as the children meet it through the activities and investigations. The teacher's notes refer to the use of the actions and noises where relevant.

The children always need to hear sentences read aloud and will then read them together as a class. In addition, all the activities stress the importance of **insisting** that the children speak a sentence aloud before they write it on whiteboards or in their books. They will also include any relevant actions and noises for punctuation. As a result, sentence writing becomes easier and more accurate.

Investigate

We believe that children understand grammar far better if they are allowed to work something out for themselves. For example, it is better to allow children to work out the 'job' connectives are doing for themselves rather than tell them. As a result, you will find that we have taken an investigative approach in some of the activities. There is often an activity designed for discussion prior to other Copymasters which require the children to apply the learning.

Use and apply

There are a number of different strategies throughout the book to help children apply their understanding:

- Card games in which they put parts of sentences together.
- A generic card game called 'Silly sentences', used throughout the book to apply learning.
- Copymasters which ask children to alter or complete sentences.
- Extension suggestions which might include writing on whiteboards or applying the learning in a different subject area.

TEACHER'S NOTES PAGE

We have arranged the teacher's notes under the following headings:

- **Objective:** This is a clear statement of the purpose of the activity.
- **Teaching point:** We have included some details about the related rules of grammar with a comment about any particular approach taken, such as auditory or visual.
- **What you will need:** This directs you to the Copymaster, which is usually on the next page. However, there are other Copymasters of nouns or connectives at the back of the book which are used with different games. Suggestions for other useful materials are made.
- **Activity:** We have suggested how you might carry out the activity on the first occasion. It is important to re-visit objectives and you will be able to create your own sentences based on the CD files.
- Where relevant, we have also included suggestions for **small group activities** or ways to further **reinforce** a learning objective.
- **Challenge:** Each activity suggests a way of moving more able children on to greater independence with writing.
- **What has been learned:** This reiterates the main purpose of the investigation, activity or game. It is important to remember to re-visit objectives on many occasions to embed learning.

CONTENTS

PART 1 – What is a sentence?
1. Rainbow sentences
2. Using full stops – 1
3. Using full stops – 2
4. Capital letters to start a sentence
5. Sentence - or not?
6. Sentence doctor
7. Missing words in a story
8. Is it a sentence?

PART 2 – Make a sentence
9. Simple sentence game – 1
10. Simple sentence game – 2
11. Silly sentences

PART 3 – Using and choosing words
12. Using nouns
13. Using proper nouns
14. Choosing precise nouns
15. Investigating adjectives
16. Using colour and number adjectives
17. Describing a picture
18. Investigating verbs
19. Choosing tense
20. Recognising tense

PART 4 – Extending and changing sentences
21. Investigating compound sentences
22. The 'and' game
23. Investigating more compound sentences
24. The 'but' game
25. Investigating connectives
26. The joining game
27. Investigating time connectives – 1
28. Investigating time connectives – 2
29. Using time connectives
30. Adding adjectives
31. Adding detail to a sentence
32. Making a sentence say the opposite
33. Alliteration
34. Similes

PART 5 – Punctuation in sentences
   35. Full stop or question mark?
   36. Asking different kinds of questions
   37. Exclamation marks
   38. Investigating commas in lists
   39. Using commas in lists
   40. Investigating speech bubbles
   41. Speech marks and speech bubbles
   42. Using speech marks

PART 6 – Additional Copymasters
   43. 'and' and 'but' cards
   44. Cards for tense
   45. Connectives
   46. Question words
   47. Punctuation sounds and actions – Year 1
   48. Punctuation sounds and actions – Year 2

1 Rainbow sentences

Objective

Identify sentences in a piece of text.

Teaching point

A sentence makes sense on its own. It starts with a capital letter and ends with a full stop. The visual aspect of this investigation will help children with their understanding.

What you will need

Copymaster 1 as an OHT or on an IAW. Coloured pens.

Activity

- Read the text on the Copymaster together. Ask children to talk about what happens next in the story of 'Goldilocks and the Three Bears'.
- Go back to the beginning and read the first sentence. Demonstrate highlighting the sentence so that it stands out. Do the same for each sentence, using a different colour each time.
- When possible, ask children to come and help highlight. Ask them how they know when to stop highlighting.
- Investigate the start and end of each sentence. What do the children notice?
- Read the text around the class and ask children to read one sentence only. Count the number of sentences as this is done.

Small group activity

- Children could each have a copy of the Copymaster and colour in their own.
- An adult with the group should ask questions to draw out the teaching points.

Challenge

- Use a piece of continuous text which does not contain conversation. In this harder example, create mistakes in punctuation and sentence sense.
- Read aloud and correct as necessary.

What has been learned

Sentences start with a capital letter, end with a full stop and make sense on their own.

1 Rainbow sentences

One day a little girl called Goldilocks went for a walk in a wood. After a while she saw a house and she walked up to look around. Goldilocks was rather a nosey girl so she pushed open the door and went in. There was no one about.

On the table were three bowls of steaming porridge. Suddenly Goldilocks felt very hungry. First she tried the big bowl of porridge but it was too salty. Next she tried the middle sized bowl of porridge but it was too sweet. Finally she dipped her spoon into the little bowl of porridge. She tasted it and it was just right. In no time at all she ate all the porridge up.

2 Using full stops – 1

Objective

To add full stops to the end of a sentence.

Teaching point

A sentence makes sense on its own. It ends with a full stop. The full stop comes at the end of the sentence, not the end of the line. The use of actions with this activity will help embed this learning.

What you will need

Copymaster 2 as an OHT on an IAW. Choice of coloured pens, sticky circles or Blu-tack blobs.

Activity

- Read the sentences on the Copymaster.
- Ask children if they are sentences. Encourage children to correct them by adding the full stops. This could be done using coloured pens, blobs of Blu-tack, sticky circles, etc.
- Introduce a 'clap' to represent a full stop. (See Copymaster 47.)
- Demonstrate reading the sentence and clapping at the end. Ask children to join in.

Small group activity

- Children each have a copy of the Copymaster and add full stops.
- They speak each sentence out loud and perform the action for the full stop.

Challenge

- Play games where you say sentences and the children have to clap in the right place. Try telling a simple story and adding in the clapped full stops.
- Read an extract from a story with no full stops, so that you do not pause for breath. Use this to help underline what the full stops are used for. (The extract on Copymaster 1 could be used for this.)
- Try putting in full stops that look like footballs – boys love this!

What has been learned

Sentences end with a full stop.

2. Using full stops – 1

Humpty Dumpty climbed up onto the wall

Goldilocks ate up all the porridge in baby bear's bowl

The first little pig built his house with straw

The big, bad wolf huffed and puffed and blew the house of sticks down

A big spider sat down next to Little Miss Muffet

Little Red Riding Hood set off to visit her Grandmother

Y1-2 Sentence Writers © Badger Learning

3 Using full stops – 2

Objective
To add full stops to the end of a sentence.

Teaching point
A sentence makes sense on its own. It ends with a full stop. The full stop comes at the end of the sentence, not the end of the line. The use of actions with this activity will help embed this learning.

What you will need
Copymaster 3 as an OHT or on an IAW. Choice of coloured pens, sticky circles or Blu-tack blobs.

Activity
- Re-read the beginning of the story on Copymaster 3. (The fact that the children are familiar with the extract from Copymaster 1 will help them concentrate on the objective of the activity.)
- Ask children if there is anything missing from the Copymaster. Encourage them to correct the passage by adding the full stops. This could be done using coloured pens, blobs of Blu-tack, sticky circles, etc.
- Ask children to remind you of the action used for a full stop. (See Copymaster 47.)
- Read the paragraph together, adding actions for the full stops.

Small group activity
- Children each have a copy of the Copymaster and add full stops.
- They speak each sentence out loud and perform the action for the full stop.

Challenge
Give the children a different section of text with missing full stops:
[the following extract can be found on the CD, 03c Sentence Copymaster Extra]

> After she had finished all the porridge Goldilocks felt tired She looked around for somewhere to sit She saw three chairs First she tried the big chair but it was too hard Next she tried the middle sized chair but it was too soft Finally she tried the baby chair and that was just right Unfortunately the chair broke
>
> So Goldilocks went upstairs to look for somewhere to sleep There were three beds First she tried the big bed but it was too hard Next she tried the middle sized bed but it was too soft Finally she tried the baby bed and that was just right So Goldilocks lay down and fell fast asleep

What has been learned
Full stops come at the end of the sentence, not the end of the line.

3. Using full stops – 2

One day a little girl called Goldilocks went for a walk in a wood After a while she saw a house and she walked up to look around Goldilocks was rather a nosey girl so she pushed open the door and went in There was no one about

On the table were three bowls of steaming porridge Suddenly Goldilocks felt very hungry First she tried the big bowl of porridge but it was too salty Next she tried the middle sized bowl of porridge but it was too sweet Finally she dipped her spoon into the little bowl of porridge She tasted it and it was just right In no time at all she ate all the porridge up

Y1-2 Sentence Writers © Badger Learning

4 Capital letters to start a sentence

Objective
To add capital letters to the start of a sentence.

Teaching point
A sentence makes sense on its own. It starts with a capital letter. The use of actions with this activity will help embed this learning.

What you will need
Copymaster 4 as an OHT or on an IAW. Coloured pens.

Activity
- Read the sentences on the Copymaster.
- Ask children if they are sentences. Encourage children to correct them by adding the capital letters. This could be done using coloured pens or by sticking over the 'mistake'.
- Introduce an action to represent a capital letter. (See Copymaster 47.)
- Demonstrate starting with the action while reading the sentence aloud. Ask children to join in.
- Play frequent games in which you say sentences and use an action for the capital letter and full stop.

Small group activity
- Children each have a copy of the Copymaster and add capital letters.
- They speak each sentence out loud and perform the action for the capital letter and clap the full stop. (See Copymaster 47.)

Challenge
- Try retelling a known story using both the actions.
- Use an extract - this time with missing capital letters. Ask children to read aloud and use the actions for capital letter and full stop.

> a little while later the three bears came up the path. they had enjoyed their walk before breakfast. daddy bear opened the door and gasped. mummy bear screamed and baby bear burst into tears.

What has been learned
Sentences start with capital letters.

4 Capital letters to start a sentence

the first little pig built his house with straw.

the big, bad wolf huffed and puffed and blew the house of sticks down.

a big spider sat down next to Little Miss Muffet.

the little girl screamed and ran away.

little Red Riding Hood set off to visit her Grandmother.

the wolf put on Grandmother's clothes and jumped into her bed.

Y1-2 Sentence Writers © Badger Learning

5 Sentence – or not?

Objective
To understand that a sentence makes sense by itself.

Teaching point
A sentence starts with a capital letter, ends with a full stop and makes sense by itself.

What you will need
Copymaster 5 as an OHT or on an IAW. Optional mini whiteboards or prepared cards.

Activity
- Read the examples from the Copymaster together.
- Ask children to give a 'thumbs up' or 'thumbs down' to indicate if they are sentences. (All the sentences have capital letters and full stops in order to concentrate on the aspect of 'making sense'.)
- As an alternative, children could write 'S' or 'not S' on a whiteboard OR hold up a card with 'sentence' on one side and 'not a sentence' on the other.
- Reading aloud is very important in this activity. Some children will 'fill in' missing words in their head to make sense and, therefore, put 'thumbs up'. It is important that they answer from what they read. Making a sentence make sense is the next starter activity.

Small group activity
- Children each have a copy of the Copymaster.
- They speak each example out loud and perform the action for the capital letter and clap the full stop. (See Copymaster 47.)
- They use ticks and crosses to indicate sentences and non-sentences.

Challenge
- Try this activity using information sentences based on the class topic.
- Speak the example aloud and ask children to indicate whether it makes sense or not.

What has been learned
Sentences must make sense by themselves.

5 Sentence – or not?

Polly put the kettle on. ☐

Humpty Dumpty climbed wall. ☐

Little Red Riding Hood met the wood. ☐

The woodcutter rushed in and killed the wolf. ☐

The second little pig built his house with sticks. ☐

Goldilocks in the little bear's bed. ☐

6 Sentence doctor

Objective
To correct 'non-sentences'.

Teaching point
A sentence starts with a capital letter, ends with a full stop and makes sense by itself.

What you will need
Copymaster 6 as an OHT or on an IAW. Marker pens. Mini whiteboards.

Activity
- Read the examples on the Copymaster together.
- Check that the children recognise these are all 'non-sentences' by asking them to give a 'thumbs up' or 'thumbs down'. (All the sentences have capital letters and full stops in order to concentrate on the aspect of 'making sense'.)
- Demonstrate how to 'mend' the first sentence. Ask children to suggest any other ways of doing it. (For example: in/inside; the/a.) They might make suggestions which change the story, for example: behind.
- Continue with the other examples. Children could discuss ideas with a talk partner first. Able children could write an idea on a mini whiteboard.
- It is important to share as many ways of correcting the sentence as possible, for example, by using alternative verbs or prepositions.

Small group activity
- Children each have a copy of the Copymaster.
- They speak each example out loud to decide if it is a sentence.
- Children work in pairs to decide how to correct the sentence. An adult acts as scribe and writes the alternatives.

Challenge
- Write some 'non-sentences' based on the class topic. Ensure that full stops and capital letters are correct.
- Ask children to make them make sense by themselves.
- Make sentence strips and ask the children to correct them using marker pens.

What has been learned
Sentences must make sense by themselves.

6 Sentence doctor

The three pigs hid brick house.

The wolf down the chimney.

Jack climbed hill.

The wolf in Grandma's bed.

Goldilocks little bear's porridge.

Frightened Miss Muffet.

7 Missing words in a story

Objective
To recognise missing words in a section of story and correct it.

Teaching point
A sentence starts with a capital letter, ends with a full stop and makes sense by itself. Full stops and capital letters are included in this activity in order to concentrate on editing a longer piece of text for sense. It is important to say a sentence before writing it to avoid missing any words out.

What you will need
Copymaster 7 as an OHT or on an IAW.

Activity
- Read the story on the Copymaster together and ask children to put up their hands when they think a word is missing.
- Take suggestions for the missing word or ask children to write suggestions on mini whiteboards.
- Re-write correctly on a flip chart or correct on an IAW, continually emphasising what makes a sentence. The added words could be highlighted in a different colour font.
- Children could continue this well known story by speaking sentences aloud.

Small group activity
- Children each have a copy of the Copymaster.
- They speak each example out loud to decide if it is a sentence.
- Children work in pairs to make corrections.

Challenge
- Use a piece of text about a class topic. Rewrite it to miss out a few words, for example: a verb, a pronoun, a definite or indefinite article and a preposition.
- Ask children to read in pairs and mark the text to show where they think the words are missing. They should speak the corrections first and then write them.

What has been learned
Adding missing words makes the sentence make sense.

7 Missing words in a story

DOES THIS MAKE SENSE?

One morning Jack's mother sent him the market in to sell their cow.

Jack a man along the road.

"I will buy cow," said the man. "I will give you bag of magic beans in return."

Jack felt very happy went home to tell his mother. She so cross with him that she threw all the beans the window.

"You stupid boy," she yelled.

Sadly, Jack to bed.

8 Is it a sentence?

Objective
To combine the previous activities and recognise a sentence.

Teaching point
A sentence starts with a capital letter, ends with a full stop and makes sense by itself.

What you will need
Copymaster 8 as an OHT or on an IAW.

Activity
- Begin by asking children how they can check for a sentence.
- Read the examples together.
- Ask children to give a 'thumbs up' or 'thumbs down' to indicate if they are sentences.

Small group activity
- Children each have a copy of the Copymaster.
- They speak each example out loud to decide if it is a sentence.
- Children work in pairs to make corrections.

Challenge
- Use a piece of continuous text which does not contain conversation. In this harder example, there are mistakes in punctuation and sentence sense:
  [the following extract can be found on the CD, 08c Sentence Copymaster Extra]

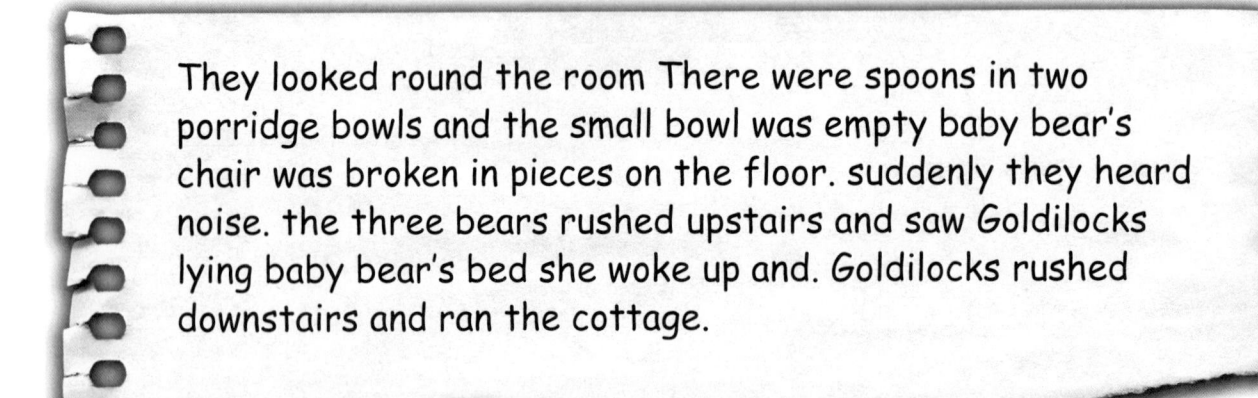

> They looked round the room There were spoons in two porridge bowls and the small bowl was empty baby bear's chair was broken in pieces on the floor. suddenly they heard noise. the three bears rushed upstairs and saw Goldilocks lying baby bear's bed she woke up and. Goldilocks rushed downstairs and ran the cottage.

- Read aloud and correct as necessary.

What has been learned
To recognise sentences by looking at capital letters, full stops and sense.

8 Is it a sentence?

Once upon a time there were three billy goats Gruff.

They lived a meadow with sweet smelling grass.

they wanted cross bridge to find more grass.

an ugly troll lived under the bridge

The troll let the little billy goat Gruff go because he was so small

the biggest billy goat Gruff butted the troll out way

Y1-2 Sentence Writers © Badger Learning

9 Simple sentence game – 1

Objective
To put two parts of a sentence together to make a simple sentence that makes sense.

Teaching point
The separate parts do not make sense by themselves. A sentence has a capital letter and a full stop.

What you will need
Sentence strips. For whole class work, enlarge Copymaster 9 and photocopy the different sections onto two different colours.

Activity
- The sentence examples on the Copymaster are all from well known stories because it is essential that children are familiar with the context in order to play the game.
- Demonstrate reading two separate parts and putting them together to make a sentence. Ask the children to read the sentence with the noises and actions. (See Copymaster 47.)
- Give out the two sets of coloured card and ask children to join them up to create a sentence. (Children could work in pairs on this activity.) Children who do not have cards help the others to find the matches.
- Ask children to stand around the room and hold their sentence so that everyone can see.
- Everyone reads the sentences and those without cards put in the actions.

Small group activity
- The game could be used again for reinforcement with a small group.
- Children make sentences from the coloured strips.
- An adult should check understanding of the three things which make up a sentence.

Challenge
- Play the game again, using sentences based on the class topic.
- Children could work in pairs and make an alternative game. They give their game to another pair to play.
- Add further challenge by leaving out some full stops and/or capital letters to reinforce those aspects of the activity.

What has been learned
To make a simple sentence by putting two parts together.

9 Simple sentence game – 1

	Goldilocks
	An ugly troll
	The first little pig
	The three bears
	The big, bad wolf
	Little Red Riding Hood

ate baby bear's porridge.
lived under the bridge.
built his house with straw.
went for a walk before breakfast.
climbed into Grandmother's bed.
went to visit her Grandmother.

Y1-2 Sentence Writers © Badger Learning

10 Simple sentence game – 2

Objective
To put the separate words in order to make a sentence and to punctuate it correctly.

Teaching point
A sentence needs a capital letter, full stop and must make sense on its own.

What you will need
For whole class work, enlarge Copymaster 10. Cut the words up and stick them onto individual pieces of card. Post-it notes and pens. Alternatively, write the separate words on mini whiteboards. (This method enables the activity to be repeated on numerous occasions with minimum preparation. Punctuation can also be added easily.)

Activity
- The Copymaster gives the opportunity to use a set of words to make a short four word sentence or several different longer sentences.
- Select the words being used and give to the relevant number of children.
- Stand them in front of the class in a random order and ask the children to read each word.
- Ask the rest of the class to organise the words to make a sentence.
- By now, children should immediately notice the need for a full stop and a capital letter. If using cards, this can be corrected by sticking on large Post-it notes. Corrections can be made easily on the mini whiteboards.
- When the sentence is complete, the children should read it aloud and use the actions for a full stop and a capital letter. (See Copymaster 47.)

Small group activity
- Photocopy Copymaster 10 and cut into strips.
- Children read the words and then sort them as a group.
- Correct punctuation and read aloud, using the clap for a full stop.

Challenge
- Play the game again, using sentences based on the class topic.
- This game can be used on different occasions to practice other kinds of sentences using the various connectives in Part 4.

What has been learned
To sort out words in order to make a simple sentence.

10 Simple sentence game – 2

he
climbed
right
to
the
top
of
the
beanstalk

Y1-2 Sentence Writers © Badger Learning

11 Silly sentences

Objective
To make up oral sentences using one or two words from the pack.

Teaching point
A sentence makes sense on its own.

What you will need
Copymasters 11a-b photocopied onto different coloured card to make two separate packs. (This is the basis for other games later in the book, so it may be useful to laminate the cards.)

Activity
- Shuffle the first pack of cards (Copymaster 11a) – subject cards.
- Fan the cards out face down and ask a child to pick one. Demonstrate how to use the word to make a sentence.
- Explain to the children that this can be as silly as they like, so long as it makes sense as a sentence.
- When the children are used to this game, introduce the second set of cards (Copymaster 11b) – objects – as well.
- Play these games little and often to constantly reinforce the idea of a sentence and to develop imaginative ideas and vocabulary.
- The sets of cards can be used later to practise using different kinds of connectives and this is mentioned in other starter activities.

Small group activity
- Play the same game in small groups.

Challenge
- Give each pair a mini whiteboard.
- Play a game as above.
- Children must speak their sentence aloud and then write it down.
- Check for capital letters and full stops.

What has been learned
To speak simple sentences aloud.

11 Silly sentences (a)

giant	elephant
spider	tortoise
monkey	witch
princess	tooth fairy
dwarf	grandpa
head teacher	mouse

Y1-2 Sentence Writers © Badger Learning

11 Silly sentences (b)

hole	jelly
potion	wellington boots
skipping rope	mobile phone
cave	motorbike
worm	ladder
pizza	lunch box

Y1-2 Sentence Writers © Badger Learning

12 Using nouns

Objective
To understand the function of nouns.

Teaching point
A noun is the name of something. It is important to choose a precise word for something. (Proper nouns are the names of people, places, important events, books and films. They need a capital letter. This is investigated in Starter 13.)

What you will need
Copymaster 12 as an OHT or on an IAW.

Activity
- Use the picture on the Copymaster as a stimulus. Ask the children to look at the scene and name objects that they see. Tell them that these are called nouns. (The picture gives the opportunity to include proper nouns after they have been investigated in Starter 13.)
- Challenge children to find alternative names for some objects.
- On another occasion, look for objects beginning with particular letters of the alphabet.

Small group activity
- Children could each have a copy of the Copymaster.
- An adult with the group should ask questions to draw out the teaching points.

Reinforce
- Repeat the activities with other pictures.

Challenge
Show the children some text. Ask them which word in bold is the odd one out and why.

> The **clock** struck twelve. Cinderella rushed out of the **ballroom** and **ran** down the **steps**. She left one glass **slipper** behind.

Repeat this using text related to topics in other curriculum areas. (It is not necessary to ask children to underline nouns. The important aspect is understanding their function.)

What has been learned
Objects are called nouns.

12 Using nouns

THINGS – AND MORE THINGS

13 Using proper nouns

Objective
To understand the function of proper nouns.

Teaching point
Proper nouns are the names of people, places, important events, books and films. They need a capital letter.

What you will need
Copymaster 13 as an OHT or on an IAW.

Activity
- Read the extract on the Copymaster together and look closely at the capital letters in bold.
- Ask the children to explain what kinds of words start with capital letters. (The extract includes examples of titles, different kinds of names, special events, addresses – including towns and countries, days of the week, months of the year.)
- Explain that they are all called proper nouns and need to start with a capital letter. Remind children of the action for a capital letter. (See Copymaster 47.)
- Look at the invitation and work together to change each of the proper nouns for an alternative. Children could have mini whiteboards and write suggestions before discussion.

Challenge
Give the children another piece of text and ask them to circle all the proper nouns.

> Christabel and Petunia were very excited. It was Wednesday so there was a lot to do. They sent a message to Ada Mopps who lived in Little Wallop. She came on Thursday and started to make two new dresses.

They could write another sentence from the same part of the story and include at least one proper noun.

What has been learned
Names of people, places, special events, days and months are called proper nouns. They need a capital letter.

13 Using proper nouns

One morning a letter popped through the letter box. Christabel opened it.

"Oh look!" she said. "It is an invitation."

She read it out.

> **Prince Charming** invites
>
> **Christabel** and **Petunia Huxton**
> to a grand **Summer Ball**
>
> at
>
> **Brockingham Palace**
> **London**
> **England**
>
> on
>
> **Saturday** 12th **June**
>
> at 8pm.
>
> There will be dancing to
> the **Big Cat Band**.

14 Choosing precise nouns

Objective
To understand the function of nouns.

Teaching point
A noun is the name of something. It is important to choose a precise word for something.

What you will need
Copymaster 14 photocopied to make a pack of cards.

Activity
- Photocopy Copymaster 14 onto coloured card and cut it up to make a pack of category cards for a word game. There are two blank cards for extra categories which are relevant to the class – for example, relating to a topic.
- Shuffle the pack and ask a child to pick a category.
- Play the game orally and generate as many nouns as possible related to each category.
- This game will reinforce the use of precise rather than general nouns.
- Create a competitive element by putting the children into teams. Each team could generate as many nouns as possible in one minute.

Small group activity
- Use the picture on Copymaster 13 as a stimulus for the traditional memory game: 'I went to the ball and I saw…' The next child repeats what has been said and adds another noun.
- Increase the challenge by asking for objects in alphabetical order!

Challenge
- Play the game as above, but ask children to write down the nouns they are thinking of. (Starters 38 and 39 deal with commas in lists.)
- If children are playing in teams, one child could be a scribe.
- Write some categories onto the back of the set of cards in order to play the same game but related to proper nouns. Categories: names, days of the week, months of the year, names of places, names of countries.

What has been learned
It is important to choose precise nouns.

14 Choosing precise nouns

animals and birds	things I like to eat
toys and games	things in the classroom
things with wheels	things at the seaside
things I might see in a magic forest	things I might find in a fairytale castle
things where I live	things in the park

Y1-2 Sentence Writers © Badger Learning

15 Investigating adjectives

Objective
To understand the function of adjectives.

Teaching point
Adjectives describe nouns. Colour words and numbers can also be adjectives.

What you will need
Copymaster 15 as an OHT or on an IAW.

Activity
- Read the pairs of sentences on the Copymaster.
- Ask children to discuss with a talk partner the job of the words in bold. Take feedback. Explain that these words are called adjectives. Refer to previous activities to help the children understand that the words are describing the nouns in the sentences.

Small group activity
- Carry out the activity in a small group.
- Reinforce using different sentences.

Challenge
- Use the cards from the 'Silly sentences' game. (Copymaster 11)
- Ask children to make up a short sentence which includes an adjective to describe the object.

What has been learned
Adjectives, including number and colour words, describe nouns.

15 Investigating adjectives

How does the word in bold help?

The wizard lives in a tower.

The wizard lives in a **crumbling** tower.

He wears a cloak and a hat.

He wears a **grey** cloak and a **pointed** hat.

He has got a beard.

He has got a **long** beard.

There is a cauldron in his workshop.

There is a **rusty** cauldron in his workshop.

Y1-2 Sentence Writers © Badger Learning

16 Using colour and number adjectives

Objective
To complete sentences using a colour or a number.

Teaching point
Colour words and numbers describe nouns.

What you will need
Copymasters 16 as an OHT, or on an IAW, or as individual copies.

Activity
- Look at the first picture on the Copymaster. Ask the children to suggest what colour the bats could all be. Colour in. Ask the children to count the objects.
- Demonstrate how to complete the sentence in two ways, using a colour or a number. Demonstrate how to speak the sentence aloud before writing.
- The children could complete the activity individually.

Challenge
Ask the children to replace the colour with an ordinary adjective. (For example: enormous bats.) Speak the sentence aloud and then write it.

What has been learned
To write sentences using number and colour adjectives.

16 Using colour and number adjectives

There are ……. bats on the ceiling.

The wizard has ……. cats in his workshop.

……. bottles stand on the shelf.

The spell needs ……. frogs.

There is a ……. cloak on the peg.

I can see ……. stars on the wizard's hat.

17 Describing a picture

Objective
To understand the function of adjectives.

Teaching point
Adjectives describe nouns. Colour words and numbers can also be adjectives.

What you will need
Copymaster 17 as an OHT, or on an IAW, and individual copies.

Activity
- Look at the partly drawn picture of the wizard in his workshop on the Copymaster.
- Demonstrate how to add to a small section of the picture in order to create detail and colour.
- Work together to generate some adjectives to describe nouns in the picture.
- Demonstrate how to label the picture. (a *bubbling* potion)
- Give the children their own copies and ask them to complete the picture to show what the wizard looks like and what his workshop contains.
- Children can generate their phrases orally and then label their picture.

Challenge
Ask the children to write a recipe for the wizard's potion using different adjectives, including colour and number. For example:

- three frogs
- one stick of green toffee

What has been learned
To use different kinds of adjectives to describe a picture.

17 Describing a picture

THE WIZARD'S WORKSHOP

Y1-2 Sentence Writers © Badger Learning

18 Investigating verbs

Objective
To understand the function of verbs.

Teaching point
Verbs show what is happening. (This starter concentrates on action that can be identified.)

What you will need
Copymaster 18 as an OHT or on an IAW.

Activity
- Look at the picture of a scene in the park on the Copymaster.
- Read the text below and discuss the job of the words in bold. Explain that they are called verbs. (This activity concentrates on the present tense only in order to focus on the function of the word.)
- Ask children to generate more verbs by suggesting other actions in the picture. Demonstrate how to give examples as a very short sentence. (The ducks swim. / The ducks are swimming.)

Challenge
Ask children to think about alternative verbs for the same action.

What has been learned
Action words are called verbs.

18 Investigating verbs

AN OUTING TO THE PARK

Sophie **throws** bread to the ducks. They **quack** and **gobble** it up. Josh **sits** in his push-chair and **screams**.

19 Choosing tense

Objective
Understand the use of past, present and future tenses. This starter will be used on separate occasions to investigate different tenses.

Teaching point
Verbs show what is happening. (This concentrates on action that can be identified.) The tense pinpoints when the action is happening. The use of actions will reinforce the idea of tense.

What you will need
Copymaster 19 as an OHT or on an IAW.

Activity
- Look at the small pictures on the Copymaster - based on the large picture of the park that the children have already looked at (Copymaster 18).
- On different occasions, introduce the children to the idea of verbs pinpointing time – past, present and future. Use the words 'yesterday', 'today' and 'tomorrow' in sentences to help understanding. Demonstrate how to say a sentence based on the picture in different tenses. When this is first introduced, concentrate on one tense at a time.
- Introduce simple actions to accompany the different tenses. For example: a thumb pointing behind; a hand held horizontally; a finger pointing forward.
- Write down the past tenses suggested and point out that many are made by adding 'ed'. Start a list of exceptions which the children can use when they write.

Small group activity
Use the Copymaster with a small group to reinforce the use of one tense at a time.

Challenge
Ask one child to say a sentence and then another to change the tense.

What has been learned
Verbs can be in the past, present or future tenses.

19 Choosing tense

ACTION – ACTION – ACTION

20 Recognising tense

Objective
Understand the use of past, present and future tenses. Recognise the tense when it is written.

Teaching point
Verbs show what is happening. (This concentrates on action that can be identified.) The tense pinpoints when the action is happening. The use of actions will reinforce the idea of tense.

What you will need
Copymaster 20 as an OHT or on an IAW. Optional - sets of cards for children from Copymaster 44. Use either past, present and future, or yesterday, today and tomorrow, depending upon the understanding of the children.

Activity
- Read through the sentences on the Copymaster, based on the story of Snow White.
- Ask the children to decide when the action is happening.
- They could do this by using the hand actions, introduced in Starter 19, or by holding up the relevant card from Copymaster 44.

Small group activity
- Children have one copy between two.
- They read the sentence and write the tense on the paper.

Challenge
- Use the three cards from Copymaster 44 with the 'Silly sentences' cards (Copymaster 11).
- Children make up a sentence in the tense indicated by the time card.
- Create more challenge by adding to the time cards. For example: now, last week, in half an hour, five minutes ago, next month, at the moment.

What has been learned
To recognise tenses in different sentences.

20 Recognising tense

PAST, PRESENT OR FUTURE?

The queen gazes into the magic mirror.

"I will be the fairest of them all!"

The servant took Snow White deep into the forest.

Snow White knocked on the door of the cottage.

She will look after the seven dwarfs.

An old woman is walking towards the cottage.

Snow White bit into the poisoned apple.

The prince kisses her and she wakes up.

Y1-2 Sentence Writers © Badger Learning

21 Investigating compound sentences

Objective
To understand the use of the connective 'and'.

Teaching point
The sentences make sense by themselves. They can be joined together with the word 'and'.

What you will need
Copymaster 21 as an OHT or on an IAW.

Activity
- Read the pairs of sentences on the Copymaster.
- Refer back to previous activities to reinforce the idea of a sentence.
- Use coloured marker pens to underline the separate simple sentences.
- Ask the children to explain the job of the word 'and' in the second sentence in each pair.
- Identify the fact that the sentence gives the same detail but there is now one sentence not two. Read the sentence aloud, using the actions for punctuation. (See Copymaster 47.)

Challenge
Investigate some pairs of sentences in which the second sentence is altered slightly. For example:

> Cinderella rushed out of the ballroom. She raced down the stairs.
>
> Cinderella rushed out of the ballroom and raced downstairs.

What has been learned
The word 'and' can join two sentences.

21 Investigating compound sentences

USING 'AND'

The ugly sisters were unkind to Cinderella.
She had to do all the jobs in the house.

The ugly sisters were unkind to Cinderella **and she had to do all the jobs in the house.**

The fairy godmother waved her wand.
The pumpkin turned into a golden coach.

The fairy godmother waved her wand and **the pumpkin turned into a golden coach.**

The prince married Cinderella.
They lived happily ever after.

The prince married Cinderella and **they lived happily ever after.**

Y1-2 Sentence Writers © Badger Learning

22 The 'and' game

Objective
To join sentences using the connective 'and'.

Teaching point
Using the word 'and' creates a longer sentence. It has a capital letter, a full stop and it makes sense by itself.

What you will need
Copymaster 22 photocopied onto two different strips of card. 'and' cards from Copymaster 43.

Activity
- Give out the sentence starts from the Copymaster and ask those children to stand at the front of the room.
- Give out 'and' cards from Copymaster 43 and the second part of the sentences from Copymaster 22 to other children.
- They join up to create longer sentences.
- Everyone reads the sentences out, using the actions for full stops and capital letters. (See Copymaster 47.)

Reinforce
- Use the 'and' cards from Copymaster 43 with both sets from the 'Silly sentences' game. (Copymaster 11)
- Play this game little and often to embed the idea of joining two parts together with the word 'and'.

Challenge
Create some more strips in complete sentences. Children have to join them with 'and' and also correct the punctuation with marker pens or Post-it notes. For example:

> Little Red Riding Hood opened the door. **She went inside.**
> The crafty wolf set off through the wood. **He reached Grandmother's cottage first.**
> The woodcutter rushed into the cottage. **He rescued Grandmother.**

Make more sentences based on class topics.

What has been learned
To join sentences using the word 'and'.

22 The 'and' game

Starts

Cinderella's stepmother shouted at her
The ugly sister put on her dress
Poor, unhappy Cinderella swept the floor
The fairy godmother waved her wand
The handsome prince saw Cinderella
The ugly sister grabbed the slipper

Ends

told her to carry on cleaning.
admired herself in the mirror.
cleaned out the fireplace.
turned six rats into coachmen.
fell in love with her.
tried to put it on.

Y1-2 Sentence Writers © Badger Learning

23 Investigating more compound sentences

Objective
To understand the use of the connective 'but'.

Teaching point
The sentences make sense by themselves. They can be joined together with the word 'but'. The word suggests a particular ending to a sentence.

What you will need
Copymaster 23 as an OHT or on an IAW.

Activity
- Read the pairs of sentences on the Copymaster.
- Refer back to previous activities to reinforce the idea of a sentence.
- Use coloured marker pens to underline the separate simple sentences.
- Ask the children to explain the job of the word 'but' in the second sentence in each pair.
- Identify the fact that the sentence gives the same detail but there is now one sentence not two.
- Read the sentences aloud, using action for the punctuation. (See Copymaster 47.)
- Discuss the meaning of the word 'but' and the kind of words which follow the connective.

Challenge
Investigate some pairs of sentences in which the second sentence is altered slightly. For example:

> The prince ran after Cinderella. He could not find her.
> The prince ran after Cinderella but could not find her.

What has been learned
The word 'but' can join two sentences.

23 Investigating more compound sentences

BUT – BUT – BUT

Cinderella wanted to go to the ball.
She did not have anything to wear.

Cinderella wanted to go to the ball but **she did not have anything to wear.**

The prince ran after Cinderella.
He could not find her.

The prince ran after Cinderella but **he could not find her.**

She pulled at the glass slipper.
It did not fit.

She pulled at the glass slipper but **it did not fit.**

Y1-2 Sentence Writers © Badger Learning

24 The 'but' game

Objective
To join sentences using the connective 'but'.

Teaching point
Using the word 'but' creates a longer sentence. It has a capital letter, a full stop and it makes sense by itself. The first part of the sentence must be followed by a 'however' kind of meaning or something unexpected happening.

What you will need
Copymaster 24 photocopied onto strips of different coloured card. 'but' cards from Copymaster 43.

Activity
- Give out the sentence starts from the Copymaster and ask those children to stand at the front of the room.
- Give out the 'but' cards from Copymaster 43 and the second part of the sentences from Copymaster 24 to other children.
- They join up to create longer sentences.
- Everyone reads the sentences out, using the actions for full stops and capital letters. (See Copymaster 47.)

Reinforce
- Use the 'but' cards from Copymaster 43 with both sets from the 'Silly sentences' game. (Copymaster 11)
- Play this game little and often to embed the idea of joining two parts together with the word 'but'.

Challenge
- Give the children the first part of the sentence and the word 'but'.
- Children complete the sentence.
- This could be done orally first and then on mini whiteboards.

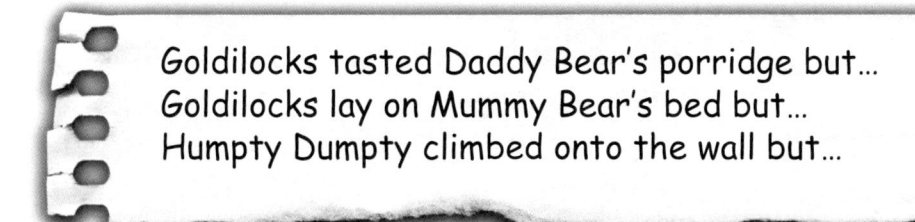

> Goldilocks tasted Daddy Bear's porridge but…
> Goldilocks lay on Mummy Bear's bed but…
> Humpty Dumpty climbed onto the wall but…

- Make more sentences based on class topics.

What has been learned
To join sentences using the word 'but'.

24 The 'but' game

Starts

Cinderella worked very hard
Cinderella asked if she could go to the ball
Cinderella longed to go to the ball
Cinderella spoke to the ugly sisters
The prince tried to catch Cinderella
The ugly sister said the slipper was hers

Ends

the ugly sisters shouted at her.
the sisters would not let her.
she had nothing to wear.
they did not know who she was.
he was too late.
it did not fit.

Y1-2 Sentence Writers © Badger Learning

25 Investigating connectives

Objective
To understand the function of connectives within sentences.

Teaching point
The connective joins the two parts of the sentence together.

What you will need
Copymaster 25 as an OHT or on an IAW.

Activity
- Read the sentences on the Copymaster.
- Refer back to previous activities to reinforce the idea of a sentence.
- Ask the children to explain the job of the words in bold.
- Use the idea of 'joining' the two parts of the sentence to reinforce the name 'connectives'.

Challenge
- Look for these connectives in reading books and class information books.
- Investigate others such as 'although'. Add them to the set of cards on Copymaster 45.
- Investigate connectives in a continuous piece of text. Ask children which word in bold is the odd one out and what job the others are doing. [The following extract can be found on the CD, 25c Sentence Copymaster Extra.]

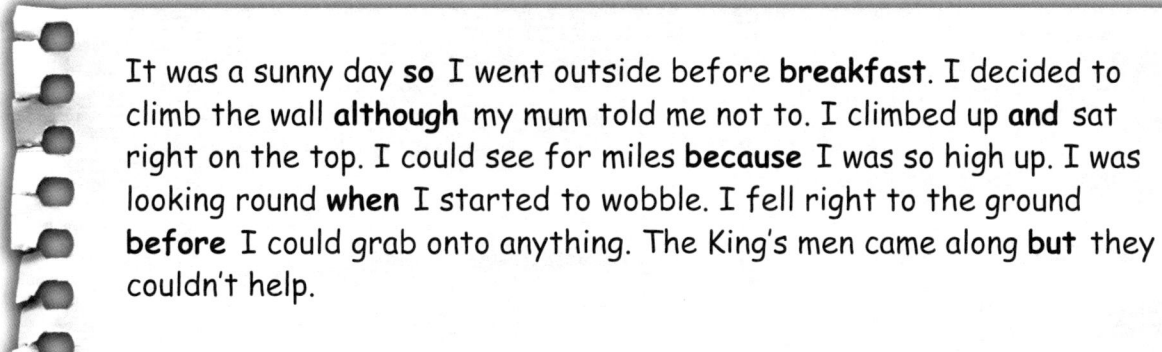

> It was a sunny day **so** I went outside before **breakfast**. I decided to climb the wall **although** my mum told me not to. I climbed up **and** sat right on the top. I could see for miles **because** I was so high up. I was looking round **when** I started to wobble. I fell right to the ground **before** I could grab onto anything. The King's men came along **but** they couldn't help.
>
> Oh dear, what a mess! I'm in hospital now.

What has been learned
Connectives join parts of the sentence together.

25 Investigating connectives

The seven dwarfs were happy because **Snow White kept the house tidy.**

The wicked queen dressed like an old woman so **no one would know who she was.**

The old woman visited the cottage while **the seven dwarfs were at work.**

The dwarfs found Snow White when **they came back from the mines.**

The prince kissed Snow White and **she woke up.**

Y1-2 Sentence Writers © Badger Learning

26 The joining game

Objective
To join sentences using a variety of connectives.

Teaching point
Different connectives help give different meaning or information in sentences. Play this game little and often to reinforce the use of a variety of connectives in different contexts.

What you will need
Copymaster 26 as an OHT or on an IAW. Set of cards from Copymaster 45.

Activity
- Read out one of the sentence starts from the Copymaster.
- Select the connectives cards (from Copymaster 45) to be used in the game and stuck around the board. There are two blank cards for other connectives which the class has investigated.
- Demonstrate how the sentence can be completed in different ways depending upon the connective used. For example: Goldilocks tasted the porridge… BUT it was too hot. *BECAUSE she was hungry.* AND ate it up. *WHEN she visited the cottage.* WHILE the three bears were out.
- Take the sentences separately – this could be on different occasions – and challenge the children to complete them using all the different connectives in turn. (It will not always be possible to use each connective with every sentence.)
- Remove the connective from the board as it is used.
- Everyone reads the sentences out, using the actions for full stops and capital letters. (See Copymaster 47.)

Reinforce
- Use relevant connectives with both sets from the 'Silly sentences' game. (Copymaster 11)
- Play this game little and often to embed the idea of joining two parts together with different connectives.

Challenge
- Make a new set of sentence starts based on a class topic.
- Children work in pairs and write the sentences on mini whiteboards.

What has been learned
To use a variety of connectives in sentences.

26 The joining game

Goldilocks tasted the porridge...

The biggest billy goat Gruff wanted to cross the bridge...

Little Red Riding Hood stopped to pick some flowers...

The wolf huffed and puffed at the brick house...

The wicked Queen gave Snow White a poisoned apple...

The ugly sisters tried on the glass slipper...

27 Investigating time connectives – 1

Objective
To understand the function of time connectives.

Teaching point
Time connectives tell us when something happened or will happen. It is important to use a variety of connectives.

What you will need
Copymaster 27 as an OHT or on an IAW.

Activity
- Read the extract from the story of Goldilocks on the Copymaster. (This is an extended version of the extract previously used.)
- Ask the children which word in bold is the odd one out.
- Ask them to discuss in pairs what the other words have in common.
- Relate back to work on connectives. Ask children what these words join up.
- Children complete the story orally, including at least four more time connectives.
- Start a list of time connectives to use when children tell or write stories.

Challenge
Give children another piece of text and ask them to underline the time connectives [the following extract can be found on the CD, 27c Sentence Copymaster Extra].

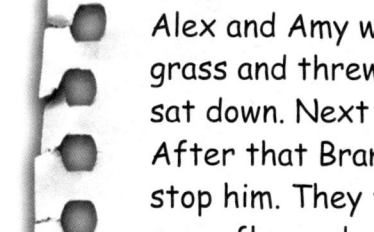

> Alex and Amy went to the park with Dad. First the children ran on the grass and threw sticks for Bramble. Meanwhile Dad found a bench and sat down. Next Alex played on the climbing frame and Amy had a swing. After that Bramble started to chase the ducks. The children rushed to stop him. They finally caught up with their dog. He was digging up some flowers!

What has been learned
Time connectives tell us when an event happened.

27 Investigating time connectives – 1

One day a little girl called Goldilocks went for a walk in a wood. **After a while** she saw a house and she walked up to look around. Goldlilocks was rather a nosey girl so she pushed open the **door** and went in. There was no one about.

On the table were three bowls of steaming porridge. Suddenly Goldilocks felt very hungry. **First** she tried the big bowl of porridge but it was too salty. **Next** she tried the middle sized bowl of porridge but it was too sweet. **Finally** she dipped her spoon into the little bowl of porridge. She tasted it and it was just right. **In no time at all** she ate all the porridge up.

A few minutes later Goldilocks sat down in the biggest chair. It was so hard that she jumped up again. **Then** she tried the medium sized chair but she sank right down in it. So she sat on the smallest chair – and broke it!

Y1-2 Sentence Writers © Badger Learning

28 Investigating time connectives – 2

Objective
To recognise the overuse of the connective 'then' and suggest alternatives.

Teaching point
Time connectives tell us when something happened or will happen. It is important to use a variety of connectives.

What you will need
Copymaster 28 as an OHT or on an IAW.

Activity
- Read the first extract on the Copymaster.
- Ask the children to discuss whether they like it or not. Could it be improved? Take feedback.
- Look at the second extract and discuss the words that could fill the gaps.
- Children could work in pairs with mini whiteboards and write their suggestions.
- Collect ideas and decide which word to use.
- Emphasise the need to choose the word for meaning and also variety.
- Add new words to the class list of time connectives.

Small group activity
Give children the second extract and allow them to work in pairs to choose suitable time connectives.

Challenge
Give children a different piece of text and ask them to carry out the same activity. In this case, children need to make some shorter sentences as well [the following extract can be found on the CD, 28c Sentence Copymaster Extra].

> Sam went to the park with his Mum and Dad and then they fed the ducks on the pond and then they walked over to the playground. Then Mum and Dad sat on a bench and had a rest and Sam played on the slide. Then he saw his friend Tom and they both played on the climbing frame. Then Mum and Dad said it was time to go.

What has been learned
To use a variety of connectives instead of the word 'then'.

28 Investigating time connectives – 2

Cinderella sat by the fire and cried. Then there was a puff of smoke and then a fairy godmother appeared.

"I will help you go to the ball," she said.

Then she waved her wand and a pumpkin turned into a coach. Then she pointed the wand at six rats and they became coachmen. Then she touched Cinderella's dress and it turned into a golden ball gown.

Then Cinderella was ready.

Cinderella sat by the fire and cried. _____ there was a puff of smoke and _____ a fairy godmother appeared.

"I will help you go to the ball," she said.

_____ she waved her wand and a pumpkin turned into a coach. _____ she pointed the wand at six rats and they became coachmen. _____ she touched Cinderella's dress and it turned into a golden ball gown.

_____ Cinderella was ready.

Y1-2 Sentence Writers © Badger Learning

29 Using time connectives

Objective
To include time connectives in different kinds of sentences.

Teaching point
Time connectives tell us when something happened or will happen. It is important to use a variety of connectives.

What you will need
Copymaster 29 photocopied onto coloured card and cut to make a pack of cards. (There are blanks for any others that the children have found in their reading. Cards from the 'Silly sentences' game (Copymaster 11) [and Copymasters 43/45].

Activity 1
- Shuffle the three packs of cards from Copymasters 11 and 29. Ask children to select from each pack.
- Children make up an oral sentence using the three words.

Activity 2
- Shuffle the three packs of cards and ask children to select from each pack.
- Add an 'and' and/or a 'but' card in order to create a compound sentence (Copymaster 43).
- Children make up an oral sentence using the four words.

Activity 3
- Use the pack of connectives (Copymaster 45) as well.
- Shuffle the four packs of cards and ask children to select from each pack.
- Children make up an oral sentence using the four words.

Different groups could practise using time connectives in different kinds of sentences at the same time. (For example, some children might concentrate on simple sentences or those joined with 'and' and 'but', while others might use a wider range of connectives to play the game.)

Small group activity
Play the same games in small groups to reinforce sentence structure and use of connectives.

Challenge
Play as above and then ask children to change the tense or use the cards to support storytelling.

What has been learned
To use different time connectives in sentences.

29 Using time connectives

First	Next
Finally	Suddenly
At last	Meanwhile
Later	After that
Soon	Once upon a time
One day	

30 Adding adjectives

Objective
To use adjectives in sentences.

Teaching point
Choose an adjective carefully. This activity concentrates on adding one adjective. Adding two is dealt with in Starter 38, related to commas.

What you will need
Copymaster 30 as an OHT or on an IAW.

Activity
- Read the sentences on the Copymaster one at a time.
- It might be useful to refer to previous work on different kinds of words. Identify these and then discuss how to describe some of them. How do the adjectives help?
- Write the children's new sentences on a flip chart.

Small group activity
- Carry out the same activity.
- Children write suggested adjectives on mini whiteboards.
- Adult scribes the complete sentence.

Challenge
- Some children, using mini whiteboards during the whole class activity, can write their own version.
- Choose one of the 'Silly sentences' games (Copymaster 11) and tell children that their sentence must include one adjective. This gives the opportunity to use the adjectives as well as different connectives.

What has been learned
To add an adjective to a sentence.

30 Adding adjectives

The prince rode on a horse.

The princess sat in the room and cried.

The stepmother led the children up the stairs.

The wizard stirred the mixture until it bubbled.

The wolf crept along the path towards the cottage.

The children saw a castle on top of the hill.

31 Adding detail to a sentence

Objective
To answer question words in order to add to a sentence.

Teaching point
Answering these questions orally will introduce children to different constructions which can be practised separately. (The question word 'who' gives the opportunity to choose names for the characters in the sentence and practise the need for capital letters for proper nouns.)

What you will need
Copymaster 31 as an OHT or on an IAW. Cards for question words – see Copymaster 46. Use one or two question words only at first and gradually introduce more question words to practise different constructions.

Activity
- Read the first sentence on the Copymaster.
- Choose one of the question words and demonstrate how to extend the sentence orally by answering the questions. For example, the word 'where' in the first example could result in… down the road/through the park/along the beach/upstairs.
- Ask children to suggest any alternatives.
- Work together on any other question words which are relevant for that sentence.
- Continue with other sentences.

Small group activity
- Ask one child to make up a short sentence based on a well known story.
- The others extend it by using the question words.

Challenge
- Write some short sentences based on a class topic.
- Use the question words to create more informative sentences.

What has been learned
To add detail to a sentence in different ways.

31 Adding detail to a sentence

The dog chased the girl.

The boy kicked the ball.

She dug a hole.

They played on the climbing frame.

Dad bought the children some ice cream.

They sat on a bench.

32 Making a sentence say the opposite

Objective
To use negative constructions.

Teaching point
The words used in the sentence must be in the same tense as the original.

What you will need
Copymaster 32 as an OHT or on an IAW.

Activity
- Read the first sentence on the Copymaster.
- Demonstrate how to make the sentence say the opposite.
- Continue with the other sentences.

Small group activity
- Ask one child to make up a sentence based on a well known story.
- The others change it to the negative.

Challenge
Play any of the 'Silly sentences' games (Copymaster 11) but tell children that the sentence must have a negative meaning.

What has been learned
To make a sentence say the opposite.

32 Making a sentence say the opposite

We are going to play on the beach.

"You can have an ice cream," said Dad.

They swam in the sea yesterday.

We will build a sand castle tomorrow.

Sam is playing in the rock pools.

I want to paddle in the sea.

33 Alliteration

Objective
To use alliteration in a sentence.

Teaching point
The sentence includes several examples of the same sound.

What you will need
Copymaster 33 as an OHT or on an IAW.

Activity
- Look at the examples on the Copymaster. Discuss the repeated sounds shown by the letters in bold.
- Work together to complete the other examples. The sentences have no full stops. This means the example can be treated as a short sentence and the full stop added. Alternatively, some groups of children could try to extend the sentence using further alliteration.
- Children could discuss their ideas in pairs before shared writing.

Challenge
- Play an alliteration game with names of people or animals. (Clever Chloe; Gorgeous Goldilocks; frisky frogs.)
- Extend to an alphabet game starting with angry ant, busy bees, etc.

What has been learned
Use simple alliteration.

33 Alliteration

The **d**irty **d**og **d**ances round the **d**ustbins.
Friendly **F**reda **f**ries **f**ish **f**or **F**red.

The _____ _____ lay

A _____ _____ tickled

The _____ _____ slipped

Y1-2 Sentence Writers © Badger Learning

34 Similes

Objective
To use a simile in a sentence.

Teaching point
A simile compares something to something else. In this activity, the examples use the word 'like'.

What you will need
Copymaster 34 as an OHT or on an IAW.

Activity
- Look at the examples on the Copymaster.
- Read each one as a full sentence.
- Ask children if they can suggest any other ideas.
- Look at another example. Children can discuss ideas with talk partners before sharing.
- Demonstrate how to write the simile as a full sentence.

Challenge
Ask the children to look for similes using the word 'like' in reading books.
Collect them for use during shared writing.

What has been learned
Include a simile, starting with the word 'like', in a sentence.

34 Similes

The triangle is like

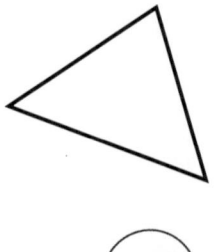

an ice cream cone

a dragon's tooth

a mountain peak

a unicorn's horn

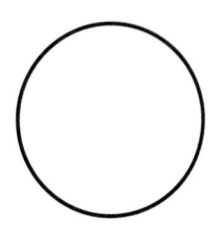

The sun is like

The moon is like

The pond is like

Y1-2 Sentence Writers © Badger Learning

35 Full stop or question mark?

Objective
To recognise statements and questions and the punctuation needed.

Teaching point
Notice different ways of starting a question. Introduce a new action for a question mark and use alongside the one for the full stop. This will help to embed the learning.

What you will need
Copymaster 35 as an OHT or on an IAW.

Activity
- Read the sentences on the Copymaster one at a time.
- Ask children if they are asking a question or just saying something in a sentence – an 'asking' or a 'telling' sentence.
- Ask children to show the action for the punctuation at the end of a sentence. Teach a new action for a question mark. (See Copymaster 47.)
- As the examples are read, children can show the type of sentence by using the action.

Small group activity
- Photocopy Copymaster 35 for individual or pair use.
- Children cut up the sentences and sort them into piles: questions and not questions.
- They can then use a marker pen and add the punctuation.
- The group should read back the sentences, using the actions.

Challenge
Use the question words on Copymaster 46 with the 'Silly sentences' cards (Copymaster 11) and ask the children to generate silly questions.

What has been learned
Full stops are used at the end of statements and question marks end question sentences.

35 Full stop or question mark?

Why did Humpty Dumpty climb the wall___

Goldilocks lay on the bed and fell fast asleep___

It is my birthday today___

Is it time to go home yet___

Do you like ice cream___

Winnie the Pooh likes eating honey___

Who is knocking on the door___

The glass slipper did not fit the ugly sisters___

When are you coming out to play___

Have you seen the wolf in the woods___

Y1-2 Sentence Writers © Badger Learning

36 Asking different kinds of questions

Objective
To construct different kinds of question sentences.

Teaching point
Questions can be asked without using question words – who, what, where, etc.

What you will need
Copymaster 36 as an OHT or on an IAW.

Activity
- Ask children to use the question starts on the Copymaster to generate questions related to a particular story or a subject.
- They speak the question aloud and match it with the agreed action (see Copymaster 47).
- Sentences can then be written on the board and re-read.

Small group activity
- Photocopy Copymaster 36 for individual or pair use.
- Children can carry out the activity above.
- They speak the sentence aloud and then write it on the sheet.
- The group should read back the sentences, using the actions.

Challenge
Use the question words on Copymaster 46 with the 'Silly sentences' cards (Copymaster 11) and ask the children to generate silly questions using the same question starts.

What has been learned
Questions can be written in different ways.

36 Asking different kinds of questions

Did you...

Can I...

Would you...

Is it...

Have they...

Y1-2 Sentence Writers © Badger Learning

37 Exclamation marks

Objective
To use exclamation marks in sentences.

Teaching point
Introduce a new action for an exclamation mark. This will help to embed the learning. This starter concentrates on exclamation marks used in speech in order to link the use of voice to the punctuation mark.

What you will need
Copymaster 37 as an OHT or on an IAW.

Activity
- Read the first sentence in the speech bubble on the Copymaster.
- Demonstrate how to read it in order to help show meaning. Teach a new action for an exclamation mark (see Copymaster 47). Add the exclamation mark on the board and read the sentence again with the action.
- Ask the children to read the other sentences, using the actions and filling in the exclamation marks.
- Encourage them to suggest what the other characters might be saying. They should speak the sentence aloud with the action before it is written on the board.

Small group activity
- Photocopy Copymaster 37 for individual or pair use.

Challenge
Ask the children to draw some more speech bubbles and write a sentence that needs an exclamation mark.

What has been learned
Exclamation marks are used at the end of some speech to show how the words are being said.

37 Exclamation marks

Please help me__

Look out__

The house is on fire__

38 Investigating commas in lists

Objective
To understand that commas are used between nouns or adjectives.

Teaching point
A comma is used between two adjectives in front of a noun. It separates the first two nouns in a list of three: -----, ----- and ------. A new action and sound is introduced in this starter to help embed the learning.

What you will need
Copymaster 38 as an OHT or on an IAW.

Activity
- Look at the first set of sentences on the Copymaster, which show two adjectives in front of the nouns. Demonstrate how to read the first sentence aloud, using the action and noise to represent the comma. (See Copymaster 48.)
- Ask the children to read all the sentences aloud.
- Explain the rule that, when two adjectives are used, a comma is put between them.
- On another occasion, look at the second set of sentences which show commas being used in lists of nouns. Use the opportunity to revise the use of capital letters for proper nouns.
- Read the sentences aloud, putting in the actions.

Challenge
Ask the children to look in their reading book to find examples of commas used in these ways.

What has been learned
Commas are used to separate a list of nouns or adjectives.

38 Investigating commas in lists

Goldilocks pushed open the small, wooden door.

The wicked, old queen spoke to the magic mirror.

The wizard wore a tall, pointed hat.

I am going to invite Ben, Jamil and Alex to my party.

We bought some apples, Rice Krispies and bread at the supermarket.

The fairy godmother collected six mice, a rat and a pumpkin.

39 Using commas in lists

Objective
To use commas between nouns or adjectives.

Teaching point
A comma is used between two adjectives in front of a noun. It separates the first two nouns in a list of three: ----, ----- and ------. A new action and sound is introduced in this starter to help embed the learning.

What you will need
Copymaster 39 as an OHT, or on an IAW, and individual copies.

Activity
- Use the detail in the picture on the Copymaster to stimulate ideas for sentences which include two adjectives or a list of nouns.
- Demonstrate how to speak one aloud and then write it. Include all the actions for punctuation. For example: Little Red Riding Hood had a cake, two apples and a pie in her basket. / Little Red Riding Hood picked up her large, brown basket.
- Children work in pairs to make up sentences. They can use the sentence starts below the picture or invent some of their own. Insist that they speak the sentence aloud before writing. (See Copymaster 48.)

Challenge
Ask the children to look in their reading book to find examples of commas used in these ways.

What has been learned
To use commas to separate a list of nouns or adjectives.

39 Using commas in lists

We bought…

I saw…

I picked up…

I looked at…

Y1-2 Sentence Writers © Badger Learning

40 Investigating speech bubbles

Objective
To understand why speech bubbles are used and recognise who is speaking.

Teaching point
The words that come out of someone's mouth are put in the speech bubble. The word 'said' is not used.

What you will need
Top part of Copymaster 40 as an OHT or on an IAW. Individual copies of the bottom part of the Copymaster.

Activity
- Look at the picture on the Copymaster and choose four children to read the speech bubbles.
- Work on the expression that would be used. Focus on the word in capital letters and how that would be spoken. Link back to the work on question marks in Starter 36.
- Children work individually or in pairs to answer the questions on the sheet.

Challenge
Look for speech bubbles in comics or reading books and explain who is speaking.

What has been learned
Speech bubbles show who is talking and what someone is saying.

40 Investigating speech bubbles

What are they saying?

I KNOW I can get it on!

You must all try on the slipper.

That will never fit! It's going to fit ME.

Can I try it on?

What is the footman saying?
What is Christabel saying?
What is Petunia saying?
What is Cinderella saying?

Y1-2 Sentence Writers © Badger Learning

41 Speech marks and speech bubbles

Objective
To make a link between speech bubbles and speech marks.

Teaching point
The words that come out of someone's mouth are put in the speech bubble. These words are put inside speech marks in stories and a speech verb is used. Using actions for speech marks will help to reinforce the learning.

What you will need
Copymaster 41 as an OHT or on an IAW.

Activity
- Ask the children to underline the words that are spoken in the first example on the Copymaster.
- Introduce some actions to represent speech marks. (See Copymaster 48.)
- Read the sentences aloud, using those actions. Emphasise the way the sentence needs to be read.
- Ask them to work in pairs on mini whiteboards and write down what should be put in the speech bubble. Check their understanding that the speech verb is not included.
- Continue with the other examples. Use the opportunity to revise punctuation. (See Copymaster 48.)

Challenge
- Ask children to suggest other things that the characters might say.
- Demonstrate how to write these on a flip chart.
- Challenge children to write an example.

What has been learned
Spoken words are put inside speech marks.

41 Speech marks and speech bubbles

"Help! I'm going to fall!" cried Humpty Dumpty.

"I will buy your cow," said the man.

"Please can I cross your bridge?" asked the little Billy Goat Gruff.

"Take this basket to your grandmother," said Red Riding Hood's mum.

"You WILL go to the ball," cried the Fairy Godmother.

Y1-2 Sentence Writers © Badger Learning

42 Using speech marks

Objective
To put speech marks around the words people say. To use question marks and exclamation marks at the end of speech.

Teaching point
These words are put inside speech marks in stories and a speech verb is used. (This activity does not focus on the inclusion of the comma, even though it would be needed.)

What you will need
Copymaster 42 as an OHT or on an IAW.

Activity
- Look at the first picture on the Copymaster and ask children to suggest what the character might be saying.
- Children should speak the sentence aloud, using any relevant actions for punctuation. (See Copymaster 48.)
- Demonstrate how to write what the children have suggested.
- Continue through the other examples, giving children a chance to write their suggestions on mini whiteboards before sharing ideas.

Challenge
Children could work in pairs as two characters from a well known story. They write a two or three part conversation.

What has been learned
To punctuate simple speech.

42 Using speech marks

43 'and' and 'but' cards

and	but
and	but
and	but
and	but
and	but
and	but

44 Cards for tense

yesterday	past
today	present
tomorrow	future

45 Connectives

and	but
because	so
when	while

Y1-2 Sentence Writers © Badger Learning

46 Question words

?	Who?
What?	Where?
When?	Why?
Which?	Whose?

If you (or the children) select the card with just a question mark, there is a free choice of question word.

47 Punctuation sounds and actions – Year 1

Full stop

Capital letter

Question mark

UH?

Exclamation mark

Wee...
bang!

Y1-2 Sentence Writers © Badger Learning

48 Punctuation sounds and actions – Year 2

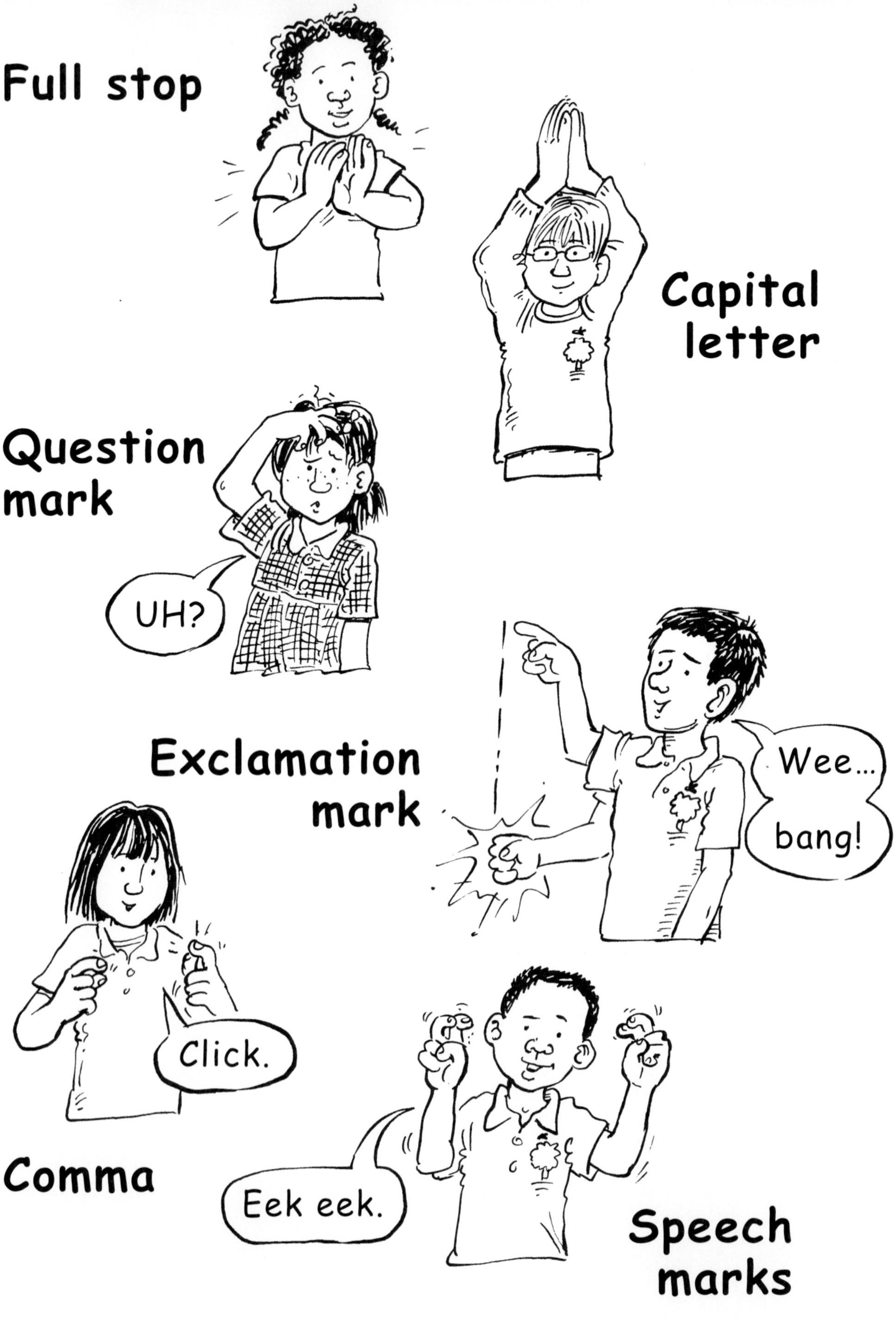

Full stop

Capital letter

Question mark

UH?

Exclamation mark

Wee... bang!

Comma

Click.

Speech marks

Eek eek.

Y1-2 Sentence Writers © Badger Learning

Badger Learning
Suite F32
Business & Technology Centre
Bessemer Drive
Stevenage, Hertfordshire
SG1 2DX

Telephone: 01438 791037
Fax: 01438 791036
www.badgerlearning.co.uk

Years 1-2 Badger Sentence Writers
Teacher Book for Years 1-2 with Copymasters and CD

First published 2007
Second edition 2013
Third edition 2019
ISBN 978 1 78837 546 7

Text © Pie Corbett and Ann Webley 2007
Complete work © Badger Publishing Limited 2019

The right of Pie Corbett and Ann Webley to be identified as authors of this Work has been asserted by them in accordance with the Copyright, Designs and Patents Act 1988.

Once it has been purchased, you may copy this book freely for use in your school.

The pages in this book are copyright, but copies may be made without fees or prior permission provided that these copies are used only by the institution which purchased the book. For copying in any other circumstances, prior written consent must be obtained from the publisher.

Note: Due to the nature of the internet, it is vital that you check internet links before they are used in the classroom.

Publisher / Senior Editor: Danny Pearson
Editor: Claire Wood
Designer: Adam Wilmott
Illustrator: Juliet Breese and Gaynor Berry

Printed in the UK